HONEYVOICED

Jordi Alonso has given us a version of Sappho in English as clean as Federico Garcia Lorca's version of Arabic poetry into Spanish: impeccably clean, each word a goldsmith gem yet flowing like the Guadalquivir River. In Jordi the words glitter as they should like Sappho's Pleiades, which after the moon and stars create the solitary intensity of palpable longing. Jordi Alonso's Sappho-inspired poems are confident works of art.

—**Willis Barnstone,** translator of *The Complete Poems of Sappho*

Since Jordi Alonso's poems are called fragments, my mind first leapt to Eliot, and the shoring against ruins. But the leap was precipitous. These rich and wonderful fragments are not bulwarks against anything, neither defensive nor resigned. They are loud, exuberant, rapacious love songs, sung by a fully-realized poet. The lines break where lyrics would. Cole Porter's, for instance. The words, so naturally right, each poem seems easy, a tune hummed on a walk. But it takes long brooding to produce work this good. That Alonso has achieved so much so early in his career makes one want to gasp. So I did, after which I sat back, closed my eyes, and gladly vanished in the music.

—**Roger Rosenblatt,** author of *The Book of Love* and *Unless it Moves the Human Heart*

This is a book of permanence: the wine-stained mouths of romantics; traces of strawberry on adventurers' hands; white linens set with indelible memories; and weather-whipped poems that are built to endure. Set against a classical backdrop, Alonso's poems bring to our current moment the passions and madnesses of the ancient world. Like the lover in one fragment, directed to carry olives down a steep incline "like you would / your love / before it has ripened," Alonso takes great care with this complex, inventive, and very welcome transport.

—**Natalie Shapero,** author of *No Object* and associate editor of *The Kenyon Review*

Jordi Alonso's *Honeyvoiced* is as sweet as it sounds. These poems will woo readers with their yearning, pleading, and seductive authenticity. A perfect read for avid poetry fans, as well as those looking for an instantly engaging entry into the genre.

—**Julia Fierro,** author of *Cutting Teeth: A Novel* and Founder and Director of The Sackett Street Writers' Workshop

HONEYVOICED
POEMS INSPIRED
BY SAPPHO'S FRAGMENTS

JORDI ALONSO

PRESS

Honeyvoiced
Copyright © 2014 Jordi Alonso
All rights reserved

Book design—Jerry Kelly
Cover photos—Jenaye Hill
Cover design—Kelly & Hill

ISBN 978-1-880977-37-8

Second edition, August 2015
Printed in USA

XOXOX Press
402 Chase Ave., Box 51
Gambier OH 43022

Visit the press at xoxoxpress.com

Library of Congress
Cataloging-in-Publication Data

Alonso, Jordi, 1991-
 [Poems. Selections]
 Honeyvoiced : poems inspired by Sappho's
fragments / Jordi Alonso. -- First edition.
    pages cm
 ISBN 978-1-880977-37-8
 I. Title.
 PS3601.L585A6 2015
 811'.6--dc23

2014039810

These poems have previously appeared in the following publications: Fragment 88 in *NEAT*, Fall 2013; Fragment 140 in *NEAT,* Fall 2013; Fragments 36, 31 in *NEAT,* Winter 2013; Fragment 40 won the Kentucky State Poetry Society Chaffin/Kash Award, First Place; Fragment 136 and Fragment 63 in *Mountain Gazette*, February 2014; Fragments 145, 192, 118, 168, 42, 141, 102, 98, 38, 99, 153, 109, 103, 20, 51, 156, 117, 160, 46, 185, 58, 127, 152, 189, 96, 6, 149, 27, and 159 in T*upelo Press 30/30 Project*, April 2014; Fragment 40 in *The Southampton Review,* Spring 2014; Fragment 55 in *The Portland Review*, Spring 2014; Fragment 192 in the *Kenyon College Alumni Bulletin*, Summer 2014

Acknowledgements

Writing, despite being touted as a solitary art, is, in my view, as collaborative as art can get. Therefore, I would like to thank quite a few people, starting with Willis Barnstone for introducing me to Sappho and for reading some of these poems while they were still in manuscript.

Sara Schultz, for introducing me to the pleasures of poetry when I was thirteen;

My parents, for their patience and support, for sending me to so many great writing workshops where many of these poems were born;

Sarah Azzara, for many things, including discovering me one summer on Long Island, and encouraging me to embrace the immediacy of poetry as a spoken art;

My tireless friend, Anjelica Whitehorne, for all she's done for *Honeyvoiced;*

Mary Ellen Walsh, for her excitement towards and support of my poetry;

Lauren Kessler, for tea, laughter, transcontinental trips, days of poetry by the sea, and a keen eye for Eros, as he appears in these fragments;

Mara Vulgamore, for nights of poetry and gin, and a friendship spanning years, reams of letters, and an understanding of each other that can only be expressed in our personal mythology of lavender-limbed nymphs and goldengreen-hearted fauns.

Meg Shaw, for many a night of sharing thoughts on writing, a bottle of wine, and countless meals and laughs;

Nina Herzog, for her love of peaches and poems featuring fruit;

Melanie Dearman, for her encouragement, friendship, great taste in art, and many lovely conversations, all which shaped many of the fragments in this book;

Emily Swaim and Katie Guyot for their insightful comments after reading the fragments in their final order;

Alan Alda, for distracting me when I needed to be distracted with many a board game, and for his kind words about my poems.

And lastly, Phoebe Carter, for her enthusiasm for languages, flowers, and poetry, for her appreciation of the erotics of food, for her love of "Fragment 88" and for being there to inspire me and to share a cup of tea, a handful of dates, and a box of chocolates when my belief in this manuscript wavered.

Introduction

No single thing first drew me to Sappho. They were several—her fame, her inaccessibility, her fragmentation, and lastly, but most strongly, her words, particularly her use of adjectives. It was that which most influenced my own style in the year in which I wrote the bulk of these fragments.

The first fragment I wrote (146) came about as a happy accident. I hadn't written anything satisfying in a month or so, and then it occurred to me that I'd take a title from another poet and write my own poem, to see if that would get me writing again. I had just discovered H.D. in an American Modernism class, and we had to read her "Fragment 116" for a Monday in April. I read it that weekend, and a day later, wrote my own version of Fragment 116 (which ended up being 146 in my numbering of Sapphic fragments).

Re-imagining that particular string of five Greek words (μήτε μοι μέλι μήτε μέλισσα) set me off on an addictive journey that resulted in over one hundred new poems, which netted me prizes, a scholarship for graduate school, and a use for my elementary knowledge of Greek. This grew alongside *Honeyvoiced* and brought me into contact with so many new people whom I now cannot imagine not knowing.

After reading as much as I could about Greek culture in the 6th century BCE culture, and particularly that of the island of Lesbos, where Sappho lived, I read every fragment of hers over and over, eventually weaning myself off from the English translations. My hope was to create not a translation, but a rewriting of Sappho, where her fragments would be stitched into my words, giving them strength and reaching for something both lovely and new. Often, I was struck by either a single phrase, and sometimes just a word in the original Greek, and I tried to bring the taste of the word into a poem in English. Along the way, I realized the potential for food and drink to signify erotic desire, and I took that concept and ran with it, weaving it into the fabric of the manuscript like a weft to guide me through to the end of the fragments.

This journey through time, place and language brought *Honeyvoiced* into focus for me. I hope you find your time with it well spent.

Note

The Fragments of Sappho are often referred to by fragment number. This apparent order has been chosen by one of Sappho's many modern editors, each of whom applies his or her own numbering system to her work. We do not know how Sappho herself ordered her poems in the nine books she produced during her lifetime, or even if she divided her work into nine books. The fragment numbers I use are, for the most part, the fragment numbers found in Edgar Lobel and Denys Page's *Poetarum Lesbiorum Fragmenta.* Because of this, even though my poems are titled after the fragments that inspired them, I have chosen to arrange them in an order fitting their emotional trajectory rather than following an imposed numerical order unrelated to the content of the fragments and not created by Sappho.

JA

for Phoebe,
because she loves these fragments—
φιλήσω

Fragment 36
for Phoebe Carter

καὶ ποθήω
καὶ μάομαι

Winter.
Wine warming,
boiling with honey, holds my hands.

With each sip
my throat heats up
and my eyes droop.

And I long and I yearn for
a spice-tongued dancer
to drink with me.

Fragment 156   χρύσω χρυσοστέρα

I am looking for a lover
sweeter than a lyre,
more golden than gold,
who will not wait
for an invitation,

but who will throw herself
into anything—impulsivity
is too-often not admired.

Fragment 126

δαύνοις ἀπάλας
ἐταίρας ἐν στήθεσιν

After grapes have been squeezed
like hands after an honest night,
and the wine of friendship poured
with no water to lessen its hug.

May you drink of the wine,
feel it numb your toes
and lighten your kisses.
May you sleep on your tender friend's breast.

Fragment 16a

Οἰ μὲν ἰππήων
στρότον οἰ δὲ
πέσδων
οἰ δὲ νάων φαῖσ᾽ ἐπὶ
γᾶν μέλαιναν
ἔμμεναι κάλλιστον
ἔγω δὲ κῆν᾽
ὄττω τὶσ ἔραται.

Long legs, and perfect form,
or dexterity famed all the way from Athens
responsible—like Helen—for war.
Which is the most beautiful?

Some say a host of cavalry, others, of infantry
and yet others of ships, is, on the black earth
the most lovely thing, but I say
it is whomever one loves.

Fragment 17   ἄγνα καὶ κάλα

I do not need as much
as I've been said to want.
My cravings today are few:
to sing with Alkaios for a night,
and a night
with a holy and beautiful virgin.

Fragment 99
for Sarah Azzara

χόρδαισι διακρέκην

The singers,
draped in white,

sip wine
to clear their throats.

Voices
refreshed,

they wet their lips;
they strike the strings.

Fragment 21   ἄεισον ἄμμι

Not of wars, politics, or dispassionate gods,
but of lust, love, home, beach, bread,
of the present,
                 sing to us.

Fragment 104a

Ἔσπερε πάντα
φέρων ὄσα φαίνοις
ἐσκέδασ' αὔως,
φέρεις ὄιν, φέρεις
αἶγα, φέρεις ἄπυ
μάτερι παῖδα.

As the sun sets,
the sky grows bright and begs
nearly every one to go home.

That is when I stretch my toes,
wash my ankles, and see
which friend of mine will host us all tonight.

Fragment 104b

ἀστερων πάντων ὁ
κάλλιστος

When you rise, Hesperos, mothers know their children
will come home. Goatherds stop
making music in the mountains:
You bring them back to the hearth
to wine, bread, and honey,
a triad they complement with cheese
brought home in bags—
warm, dripping with whey.

Fragment 82

εὐμορφοτέρα
Μνασδίκα τὰς
ἀπάλας Γυρίννως

Mnasdika is more beautiful than soft Gyrinno,
Andromeda more metrical than Kydro,
Gongyla, heart-ripper, more lovely than Megara,
    but Atthis is loveliest and best.

Fragment 146

μήτε μοι μέλι μήτε μέλισσα

Neither the honey, nor the bee
that makes it, nor wine or bread
fresh-risen from the oven
topped with crumbled cheese
will be enough to calm my hunger.
No, I am not ravenous, though you might think
I am. In fact, the smallest crumb would satisfy me:
a light whisper would be all I'd want to drink,
the warmth of hair beneath my hand would be
my loaf of bread, and if I wanted something
slightly sweeter, a kiss would be
my after-dinner date.
I will have neither honey
nor the bee that makes it.

Fragment 20

ἔλοισι ναῦται
μεγάλαις ἀήταις

To want a body
next to mine in bed
is to reason with the sea.

We sailors cannot say
where this wind will move us,
we can only hope for land.

Fragment 86   Κυθέρη'εὐχομ'

Kytherea, pray for me
though I haven't worked your bronze
into gleaming swords
or shining shields fit for Achilles,
I have taken your burnished ground
and sang for it, for friends and lovers.

Fragment 33

χρυσοστέφαν'
Ἀφρόδιτα

Foam-born Aphrodite,
Cyprian,
mother of Eros,
let me achieve my goal,
Paphian,
Kytherea,
gold-crowned Aphrodite.

Fragment 134

ζά τ' ἐλξάμαν ὄναρ,
Κυπρογένηα

In a dream, I spoke to you,
Cyprus-born, the Aphrodite
of my circle of friends.
And I asked what I might do
to persuade you to let me
return to that rich island
where burnished copper flows
from the heads of garlanded girls.

Fragment 71   μέλος τι γλύκερον

What would I need
to be happy
but the tentativeness
of a touch,
the slyness
of a kiss,
a sweet song
and the thought
of you,
brushing your hair
with your hands?

Fragment 96   ερον

I shall enter desire
desiring—

desiring to desire
and having desired

that my desires
coincide with yours:

a sweet fig
dripping nectar,

a cool bath
easing the summer,

a soft kiss
lifting my worries.

Fragment 127
for Meg Shaw

δεῦρο δηὖτε Μοῖσαι

They made me promise
to give them everything
I had in exchange for a honeyed tongue.

I have no Lydian gold,
no Egyptian love
charms, nor any emeralds from across the ocean.

Come to my table,
and I will swear off the Muses,
singing only for you:
we'll share sweet quince,
cheese seared over applewood,
and figs, waiting to be broken.

Fragment 184   κίνδυνος

To listen to your voice
is a danger
I will relish.

For a word,
for a promise,
for a touch

of your hand
I will vow
never to love

if it allows
me to sit
by your bed.

If your hands
were to linger
on my face,

and your words
flood my ears
with our wants,

I would quiet
you with kisses,

tasting pepper
and my hunger
on your tongue.

Fragment 119

αἱμιτύβιον
στάλασσον

I would give
not a kingdom,
but a basket of figs,
not to be yours,
but to be a dripping napkin
pressed between your lips
on a hot day after you've eaten a peach.

Fragment 112   ὄππατα δ' μέλλιχ'

Your tongue is a fig,
soft and refreshing,
your lips, cherries,
red and tart,
your eyes honey,
molten, warm.

Fragment 40

κἀπιλείψω τοι

I will pour
dark red wine
when you need
the soft touch
of the grape

as you lie
on my couch,
when you want
me to sing
we will drink

and our lips
will be stained;
I will pour
dark red wine
when you ask.

Fragment 105

γλυκύμαλον

Be loving:
Eros burning for a butterfly.

Be irresistible
undiluted wine from Chios.

Be beautiful
like the song-raised walls of Thebes.

Be comforting,
spiced milk when the stars are cold.

Be teasing,
a promise of a new song from an old friend.

Be flirty,
singing of the laurels you have frozen.

Be surprising,
a sweet apple in an unripe bushel.

Be adventurous,
taste the lips of laughter.

Fragment 51

οὐκ οἶδ' ὄττι θέω,
δύο μοι τὰ
νοήμνατα

Should I get the girl I want
to taste the daughter of the vine

so that I might take
her home?

I don't
know what to do

two words
spring up

yes; no.

Fragment 30   νύκτ

No sleep, tonight, for us
who—Bacchic—pour the
dark red wine from cup to throat.

No sleep for us tonight
who kiss the wine-stained
tongues of girls and taste their smoke.

Fragment 43

ἀλλ' ἄγιτ', ὦ φίλαι,
ἄγχι γὰρ ἀμέρα

The strumming of the lyre
brought pleasure to us,

wrapped in the humid hugs of summer
our tongues flitted

and the sheen of Eosphoros
passed by unnoticed.

Morning is a thankless time:
the sun vies for attention with our beds

or signals the end of a night
of Maenadlike pleasures.

There is more to drink and less to care about;

there are still unkissed lips
that will linger tomorrow,

clothes to be tossed off
with anxious excitement—

but let's go, dear friends,
dawn arrives at the party.

Fragment 46   μολθάκαν τύλαν

I can't know
when my mind
will find love.

I won't tell
when it does
but I'll bake

enough sweets
so the wind
tells you all

with its scent.

If you smell
cardamom,
know she dances.

If there's rose
in the air
we'll have kissed

and the cushions
on her couch
will be soft.

Fragment 149

ὄτα πάννυχος ἄσφι
κατάγρει

Let me curl
at your feet
while you spin
stories from
cherry stems;

let's entwine
our tongues
until dark sleep
closes our eyes.

Fragment 58   κάλον καὶ νέον

Though you have felt
the giddiness of love
tingling in your throat
like my face
after too much wine,
I have hope
that when we kiss
and clasp our hands together
you will say
our hunger is both
lovely and new.

Fragment 213

χλωροτέρα δὲ
ποίας εμμι

I am greener
than grass

when it comes to
the fashions of loving.

Weather me, sweetheart,
run on me, a field in Eressos

where unpicked violets bend
under your feet, scenting your heels with oil.

Dig through my soft dirt
and plow me. I will be fertile,

plumping dates
for you to feed your sweet tooth.

If you're thirsty, impatient
for wine to be pressed,

find my spring,
and peel a pear,

(it may be green and firm,
but sweet, cupped in your hands)

I wouldn't let you
hunger for its flesh.

Fragment 163   τὸ μέλεμα τὦμον

While I wait
for the harvest,
for the amphorae of wine
at my storehouse
to be opened,
for the salted air—
for my hair
to be wind-whipped
like a tender laurel sapling
in a rainstorm,
for you to come to Mytilene
from Eressos, to cross our island
so that we might eat
dripping honeyed almonds
and bring color to our eyes
with Methymnean vintages,

my breath catches in my throat—my voice
ragged from singing of your loveliness,
and I wonder what you'll say
when I ask you to be
my beloved.

Fragment 32

αἴ με τιμίαν
ἐποηεσαν ἔργα
τὰ σφὰ δοῖσαι

You ask why I'm so good.
Apollo kissed me, so did Aphrodite:
he kisses every poet, she the best.
His lilting lyre lights the Lesbian lands.
He gave me the secret of his work,
and doing so, made sure I honor her.

Fragment 133

Ψάπφωι, τί τὰν
πολύοβον
Ἀφροδίταν

I came

to lessen the pressure of my mind:

a covered pot of boiling water.

And even then, you said,

as you added wood to the stove:

"Sappho, why ignore many-gifted Aphrodite?"

Fragment 56
for Lauren Kessler

οὐδ' ἴαμ δολίμωμι
προσίδοισαν φάοσ
ἀλίω ἔσσεσθαι
σοφίαν πάρθενον
εἰς οὐδένα πω
χρόνον τέαυταν

When you rose
out of the crowd
as if out of a shell
in the ocean of Cyprus,

when you sang,
ink still smeared
on your fingers,

when you woke
tangled in unwashed sheets
cleaned by the salt of the air,

when you played
in the moonlight
with the words

I had whispered,
I said: "I do not think
that any girl
who has seen the sun
will have your charm,
or such skill
at any time
in the future."

Fragment 185b   μελλιχόφωνοι

If you come to me
with a scarf draped
round your neck
when mine is bare—
when my throat is sore from singing,
softvoiced, I'll send you away

returning to my kinder friends.

Drape it around me
or bind my hands to yours—
tightly
so they're whitened
by the purple silk
and I'll throw those lovely girls away

and kiss you deeper for it.

Fragment 27   μέλεσθ'

I will sing Aphrodite
of the covered kisses
had at midnight
through summer silk
though the hearth was cold
and the unpicked figs
hung heavy on their branches.

Fragment 125

αυταόρα
ἐστεφαναπλόκην

In my youth, I wove garlands
bending the lily with the daisy,
the hyacinth with the violet,
draping ropes of flowers on my friends and lovers.

But now, knowing the Muses
I don't busy myself with flowers—they wilt.
Instead, I sing garlands of words,
fresh forever in their black stems.

Fragment 154   ἐφαίνετ' ἀ σελάννα

The moon appeared
as the flower-weaver strung her garlands

as the priestess of Knossos sung a hymn to Aphrodite
the moon appeared.

Fragment 153

πάρθενον
ἀδύφωνον

When I drink water
and my throat is washed,
I forget the mysteries of taste.
You are a sweet-voiced girl—
when you laugh,
when you sing,

when you talk,
I long to touch your lips
on mine, and remember spiced honey.

Fragment 2

χρυσίαισιν ἐν
κυλίκεσσιν

My lady of Kypros,
like the men who drink wine
and mix it in bowls
with water from the whispering stream,
leave the round grape of Dionysos,
pouring instead honeyed nectar
into golden wine cups:
a full-strength toast to Eros.

Fragment 138   στᾶθι κἄντα φίλος

A light touch,
quick thought
and the gift of you—
your dripping words
are my bread and olives.

Stand before me if you love me.
I'll reach out my hand
and weave my fingers with yours.

Fragment 104c θέλω

I want
a warm droplet of honey on my tongue,
to kiss you after your song has ended
by the table where the wine is mixed with water.

Fragment 60 μάχεσθαι

Faced with a phalanx
of interlocked shields
and horsehair-plumed helmets,
I wouldn't want you to stare
with anger at the strength of others.
Purse your lips, think of love,
fight for me,
and take me as your spoils.

Fragment 18

πάν κεδ
ἐννέπην
γλῶσσα μ᾽
μυθολογῆσαι

Everyone says I lie,
that my tongue wags
inventing stories
for my benefit,

and I reply:
"oh, tongues will wag,
and wagging,
flutter beautiful words."

Fragment 41

ταὶς κάλαισ' ὔμμιν
τὸ νόεμμα τὤμον οὐ
διάμειπτον

Whether you ate an orange—
bitter and puckering,

or an almond
clear and moonlit,

lovely,
I'll crave you.

Fragment 141 κῆ δ᾿ ἀμβροσίας μὲν

Dip into me
and ladle me onto you
when the moon
reflects the sea.

Fragment 34   κάλαν σελάνναν

Your friends are stars
among the darkness of night,
guiding sailors to bed,

but you are the lovely moon;
I look to you for comfort
not caring if the morning star will rise.

Fragment 121   ἀλλ' ἔων φίλος ἄμμι

Lie with me
until our skin
is sea-scented
and the ridge
on the roof
of our mouths
is dry.
Let the sun
simmer the sea
as I have simmered for you.

Fragment 108

ὦ κάλα, ὦ χαρίεσσα κόρα

Let me taste your skin
after you have dipped into the sea
so my lips are salted with morning,

lovely and graceful.

Let me touch your hands
after you've kneaded dough
so I have the strength of wheat.

Fragment 52

ψαύην δ' οὐ
δοκίμωμ' ὀυράνω
δυοπαχέα

I should not hope to touch
the sky with my two arms
if I have yet to explore
the shape of the earth—
your shape—with both my hands.

What do I care if the moon
is unreachable?
Her slowly blinking eye
holds less promise for me
than your mouth as it opens and closes.

Fragment 156

γάλακτος
λευκοτέρα

What do I care
if you've tanned in Sardis,
or by the beach?

I can't deny my wants,
or blame the color
of your skin—I want.

If your thighs
are whiter than milk
what will I do?

I will lap at them
in the morning
like a hungry cat.

Fragment 102

γλύκηα μᾶτερ, οὔτοι
κρέκην τὸν ἴστον
πόθῳ

How can I work
when a lovely girl
dips cherries in honey
and lays her finger
on my lips?

Fragment 109   δώσομεν

We shall give
to our loves
all we have:

cakes baked in the morning
strewn with violets,
scented with cardamom,

purple plums
picked from the slopes
of Parnassos,

and fresh figs
heavy and dripping,
split with our fingers.

Fragment 136   ἄγγελος... ἀήδων

Because the snow melted,
because your sandals pressed down on soft earth,
because you said we should plant basil–

because you came to my house
after braiding your hair
with chrysanthemums

and your lips were cold.
You thawed and you said
you had never been kissed.

When you breathed
I knew you were
the herald of spring.

Fragment 16b

πόας τέρεν ἄνθος
μάλακον μάτεισαι

When the dew perched
by each blade, a lead drop
protecting dancers' feet from pain,
dawn lit the way,
and barefoot, you stepped lightly
crushing the soft flowers of grass.

Fragment 185a μελίφωονοι

Your warmth is nutmeg-scented

in the morning, when I want of a kiss,
but would accept a brush of your hand
exploring

with a tentative touch
like trembling fingers
of feather.

Honeyvoiced,
you make me long
for a hungry lover.

Fragment 152
for Nina Herzog

παντοδάπαισι
μεμειχμένα
χροίαισιν

When you brought home
a basket of strawberries

red and bright
like the tongue
that would taste them

I would have said
how lovely they were,
but your hand dipped

and raised one to your lips—
and your tongue swirled
around the seeds

when you bit into summer,
staining your fingers.

Fragment 169 ἀγαγοίην

I might lead
you astray if
we hold hands,
if we kiss,
and my muse
might be jealous.

Fragment 110   σάμβαλα

So what if it's late
and we've been here too long,
swirling the sediment
of this wonderful wine
in our cups?

So what if the cherries
we were going to pluck
in the morning are gone
and the lamp is dying
and I've lost a sandal?

There are worse things.
The wine is on the table
and our cups are empty.
Before it sours,
let's drink while there are stars
to hide us from the morning.

Fragment 45   ἄς θέλετ' ὔμμες

As long as you want
to make this summer last,
I am yours—
for as long as you want.

Fragment 1

αἰ δὲ μὴ φίλει,
ταχέως φιλήσει
κωὐκ ἐθέλοισα

Once I've offered up my prayer to Aphrodite
you will lay your hands on my head,
touch your many-colored rings to my hair.

Love, her specialty, should not be left
to chance. I'm not an amateur—three names
ensure love: Tyche, Eros, Peitho,

and one of them, if he is kind,
will petition Aphrodite.
Let the sea foam froth an answer:

Take it step by step, Sappho,
you know Artemis has the right idea in hunting
(though she's still a virgin).

And the goddess will brush
her copper ringlets from her face
and I will have seen bare beauty

more lovely than the seashells
polished by the girls who burnish
the sand of Eressos away—

I will have seen beauty bare
her head and I will have worn
her crown of chrysanthemum.

Only Erato the singer,
or the geometers of far-off Athens
could more easily approach perfection.

In the eye of any storm that rattles these islands
passion will be born, as you were,
and flicked back, like seawater

frothed by the waves, but I will keep
my faith in the foam of the sea,
since I know its white flecks will answer me.

How will I make her love in me
what is worthy
and unworthy of love?

Sappho, using your art,
your soft voice growing harsher,
seductive, coy, or happy,

say what she'd blush to hear,
what she'd smile to know,
what she'd long to taste.

Let her know who you are:
Sappho of the holy tongue,
Sappho of the sweet laugh,

and if she did not love you before,
soon she will love you,
even unwillingly.

Fragment 22

ὡς ἄραμαι
τοῦτο τὤπος
βόλλομαι

My mind is fickle—
as a singer, I encourage emotion.
I can't help it if one day a week
another girl catches my eye.

I may write some lines
about, or to her, but
you know:
infidelity is healthy in an artist.

Love once blamed me
for saying two words
too often, two short words
in a shorter time:
I want.

Fragment 117   ξοάνων
for Lauren Kessler

When the time
comes for us
and our words
to mingle in the ocean,

when we want
to linger on the sand
tasting strawberries—
lulled into beauty
by the soft-beating sea

we will rule
our fantasies of fame
not with rough untuned fists,
but with smooth singers' hands.

Fragment 65   Ψάπφωι, σὲ φίλεμμ᾿

Aphrodite, dipping her fingers in honey
allowed me to sit by her side,
and I wished my lips were coated. She said,
"Sappho, I loved you
best, so I found a singer
to soothe your ears.
Let her lyre wake you
from uncertain sleep.
She has two oceans in her voice,
and your eyes are coral reefs."

Fragment 103a   ἄγναι Χάριτες

I will let the holy Graces spin
my thread, not needing three spinster sisters
to weave, and measure out, and cut
my life short when they've tired of me.
I have three sisters. I will thank them,
remembering their kindness. The Pierian Muses
gave me this lyre—I will give them song.

Fragment 143

χρύσειοι δ'
ἐρέβινθοι ἐπ'
ἀιόνων ἐφύοντο

We walked along a river in Boeotia
shaded by almond trees.
Having bathed with you in the Pierian Spring,
we looked for ways to sing no matter what.
Hyacinth and asphodel sprouted by the water,
and golden chickpeas grew on the banks.
Thetis dipped Achilles in the Styx
but missed his ankle. Under the shadow of Parnassos,
I made sure to doubly wet your feet
and have you drink the water—coat your throat
to never have it sore or have your voice
be too soft for Melete and Aoïde.
And you pushed me off the riverbank.
My dress was soaked, and now my voice is stronger.

Fragment 147

μνάσεσθαί τινά
φαιμι καὶ ἔτερον
ἀμμέων

When we have lost count of the kisses
and the wines we have tasted,
forgotten the feeling of freckled faces,
the scent of love and honeyed almonds,
and the sound of our singing,

breathe, holding my hand, and know
someone will remember us in the future.

Fragment 7 φίλα

My love,

if the narcissi
we hung up
have drooped and dried,

and the room
where we kissed
no longer

is scented
with lilies,
let's take

the dried blossoms
and crush them—
clasping hands.

Fragment 44

Φοίβωι χρυσοκόμαι

Gold-haired Phoebus,
Lyred laureate,
let my plectrum
pluck chords—
let my hand
strum strings—
let my heart
keep time.

Fragment 166

φαῖσι

They say
the marble of Paros
is the best,

but you are whiter and smoother.

They say
Attic honey
sweetens tongues

but you are sweeter and taste like violets.

Fragment 58

ἔρος τὠελίω καὶ τὸ
κάλον λέλογχε

Spraying your face
like the seadrops
which I taste guiltily
on your lips,

the bright delicacy of the sun
is both sharp
and comforting.

Fragment 25

ὠς δὲ πάις πεδὰ
μάτερα
πεπτερύγωμαι

Not for your kisses, but for the warmth of your hugs
have I flown to you like a child to her mother.

Fragment 63   ὄνοιρε

Sleep, let your legs
sprawl with mine.
Let my lips plow
the light fuzz of your belly.

Dream of the ocean,
of driftwood fires on the shore,
of freshly gathered clams.

Let me till
moon-grown figs
in the morning.

Fragment 192   χρυσαστράγαλοι

I had to eat
with my eyes
as you took
a ripe peach
from the bowl
and its skin
scented yours

and I thought
we should kiss
when you bit into it,
when you licked
at the cleft
and its juice
wet your chin.

Don't clean
off your fingers
on the linen,
there is silk
in my room
and rosewater in
gold-knobbed goblets.

Fragment 6   στεῖχε

Fill
these jugs with sweet wine
from Methymna.

Go,
so that we may see
what gold the Lydians have to sell.

Fragment 103b   φερην

Carry
this basket of olives
down the steep terrace
like you would
your love
before it has ripened.

Fragment 148

ὁ πλοῦτος ἄνευ
ἀρέτας οὐκ ἀσίνης
πάροικος

I would not want you
to count coins

if that were your only
road to joy.

Blend wealth and wit,
(warm milk and cinnamon)

and spend them, instead, on us,
as if they were kisses

and we will wear gold sandals
and scent our house with cloves.

Fragment 4   γχροΐσθεις ἔρος

When I wear
the Lydian headband

that you found
at the market,

when I wrap
my sandals around

my sunburnt ankles
which you'll soothe

with cold oil,
I'll love you.

When I wash
the white dress

that you wove,
stained with love,

by the river
in the morning,

we will kiss
in the water.

Fragment 160   κάλως ἀείσω

Press your palm
to mine and let me
linger on your tongue—
I will sing beautifully—

when I kiss
the red poppy
whose petals flutter
on my lips—

take my hand—
if you ask
me to have you
I will—

sing beautifully
of me if you find
beauty enough
to keep for yourself.

Fragment 27

μέλεσθ' ἄγι ταῦτα

I would not ask
the Muse to sing for me
if she filled my mouth
with burnished bronze,
history, and swift-footed men.

I want glory. I want my name
to be tasted on the tongues of singers
when my voice has broken.

Don't sing of rage, Muse,
but of madness, love, and want,
of beaches, seas, and dates.

Fragment 140   τί κε θεῖμεν

What should we do
when the girl we would have held,
the lips we would have touched,
and the honey with which we would have baked
are gone?

We will not ask
for a conciliatory hug;
kisses in the autumn—out of the question.
The bread can be counted on to rise
dressed in crystals of sea salt.

Fragment 31

ἀλλὰ κὰμ μὲν
γλῶσσά μ' ἔαγε

I want to say "I love"
when I see him
talking to you
and he gives
you a date.

I should drink
so the water
I cup in my hands,
cold from the spring,
soothes and drowns me.

I am crushed
against the stucco
of your house
when he whispers
and you laugh.

I look at you,
an uneaten pomegranate,
red-ripened—
my throat cramps.
I look down.

I want to whisper "love"
but my tongue has snapped:
my lips are dry,
a subtle fire
burns my voice away.

Fragment 5

καὶ φίλοισι ϝοῖσι
χάραν γένεσθαι

Lead the way
with your kithara for me,
let your sisters know
that while I love them,
I love you the most.
Erato,
mother of joy.

Fragment 37 ἔμον στάλαχμον

My pain drips
like the wine, poured
by the shaking host
who wouldn't dare
lose one drop
to the ground,
who wouldn't wish
harm to the vine
by spilling the bitter
blood that makes us
stumble, laughing into
gritty walls drawing
our own less lovely
life, staining white linen.

Fragment 137

θέλω τί τ᾽ εἴπην,
ἀλλά με κωλύει
αἴδως

I want to memorize your songs to honor the Muses
        but I can't focus on letters;

I want to walk beside you by the market
        but you always walk with other girls;

I want to brush your purple hair at night
        but you are far away and I'm alone;

I want to say something to you
        but shame won't let me.

Fragment 130   γλυκύπιλρον

When she walks by the persimmon-tree
and takes an orange globe,
biting into its firm sweetness,
when she buys a book and giggles,
when she plays the flute, trilling
a happy melody, listening raptly,
Eros, limb-loosener,
tongue-tightener, shakes me
and a sweetbitter taste floods my mouth.

Fragment 139   ἀδάκρυτον

Though I may sing
to an empty couch
while I wait
for my lover
alone,

my voice will not waver
my hands will be steady—
I will not brine
my face with tears.

Fragment 42

μὲν ἔγεντ᾽ ὁ θῦμος

Why should I wait
for a word from a love
if her head
no longer rests
on my shoulder
and her heart has grown cold?

Fragment 8   σο

I walked outside to pick herbs
to bake with, to burn,
to taste alone
when I want
to forget a lover.

My lips should taste
like mint and I
can't find
a sprig
comparable to you.

A bed for two stands
unmade in the morning—

Fragment 57

οὐκ ἐπισταμένα τὰ
βράκε᾿ ἕλκην ἐπὶ
τὼν σφύρων

I thought you were
alone for now—I know
I am. I can curl up in bed

without your bony shoulders
digging into me—without you,
who will question that I'm the better singer?

I can swim in the bay of Antissa
where Orpheus once kissed the sand,
and the sea salt spices my singing.

Where have you been,
cut off from the company of singers?
I hear you've gone home.

What farm girl feeds your fantasies,
dressed in rough fabric
not knowing how to pull her rags down to her ankles?

Fragment 118
for Melanie Dearman

ἄγι δὴ χέλυ δῖα μοι
λέγε
φωνάεσσα δὲ γίνεο

I would follow you
to the house of Hades
like Orpheus,
and I would tear down
the walls of Thebes
with a furious strumming
of my lyre
if I could keep you by me,
and keep wet, warm sand
glinting between our toes.

Fragment 145   μὴ κίνη χέφαδος

Do not move stones
when they are whole;
hearts are easily moved
once they have broken.

Fragment 94

πόλλοις γὰρ
στεφάνοις ἴων καὶ
βρόδων κροκίων

I'll let you go with a wreath of crocuses.
Like our love,
they too will wilt.

Fragment 98

σοὶ δ᾽ ἔγω Κλέι
ποικίλαν
οὐκ ἔχω πόθεν
ἔσσεται μίτραν

In exile

nothing remains of the taste

of Lesbos—sweet wine,

coarse salt, and fragrant rosewater

no longer coat my tongue,

my lips, my fingers.

I have no silver to buy Sicilian dresses;

my crimson chithon tattered last week

and I had hope. I gave it to Cytherean Aphrodite.

I'm dressed in white. My hair held back

by a bronze lyre—I can't let go.

They call Apollo Mousagetes here
as well, and I had faith he'd lead me to my sisters.
Bring me back to you.

Atthis, if I could, I'd send you a harp
and a plectrum carved from the rock of the Cyprian,
so you'd forever be beautiful and clear-voiced.

Dika, there is a chestnut tree
on the slope of Mount Etna
with white flowers.
If you're tired of the anise
you twine in your hair,
I'll pluck them for you.

Andromeda, I would not think of sending you an olive branch,
instead, a kylix made from the clay
I gathered by Arethusa's cave, so you too, can drink song.

Lovely golden flower, you are last—
come join me soon—I feel alone without you.
I can't make the world die for your absence
but I'll ask Gelos, after some wine,
to keep you laughing.

For you, Kleïs,
I have no embroidered headband
no gift at all but a kiss, from singer to singer.
Pray to your father, the leader of the Muses, to bring you here
and I will unwind gold thread to guide you home.

Fragment 159   κακοζοΐας

If a pot of beeswax
to soothe lips
chapped from sun and smiles,

a thin reed,
whose once sharp tip is worn down,
blackened with soot,

and a sherd of baked clay
incised with the words
"I will love"

are seen
as the relics
of a wretched life

may the marble-carved
virtues of men splinter
like Zeus' head

when the world
welcomed
his daughter.

Fragment 157   Αὔως

What use is there for a shepherd
blindly wandering at night
holding his boy's hand
while dark wine spills
from his lips?

I can see at dawn
and stand alone
over seafoam,
and my tongue
tastes of strawberries.

Fragment 55

ἀφάνης κἀν Ἀίδα
δόμῳ

When you have popped
the last fleshy olive
into your mouth
and thrown away the pit
at the foot of some hungry girl,

when you are dead
and your bones have been bleached
by the grapes growing over you,
sapping your life into their skin
to be crushed, as you should have been,

there will be no crying over food,
and no one will say your name with love
when we gather for a summer night,
chatting over stuffed grape leaves. You'll be unseen
here and in the house of Hades.

Fragment 150

οὐ γὰρ θέμις ἐν
μοισοπόλων οἰκια

Pause if the one you love says no. Then breathe. Sing.
It is not right that there be tears in the house
of those who serve the Muses.

Fragment 188

μυθοπλόκον

Although my eyes see clearly
when others are rejected in love,
I dream of myself as unmovable.
Wayward love is a tale-weaver,
stale wine folded in honey.

Fragment 162   τίοισιν ὀφθάλμοσιν

How will you judge
if my apple is the best?
With what tongue
will you taste its tartness?

With what hands
will you hold my throat,
what fingers by my earlobe
will feel me sing?

With what eyes
will you see that I dance
for my friends,
not for you?

Fragment 182   ἰοίην

When the nereids dance
around the oak
that the storm uprooted

I might go to the laurel
and think of dedicating myself to it.
But oaks are strong;
look at this hardy sapling.

Fragment 171   ἄκακος

Some say Love is evil,
making us want unachievably,
buffeting our hearts
like the lone laurel
atop the Leucadian Cliffs.

But I say
we grow stronger,
roots reaching deeper.
Love is rough like cold rain
and unevil.

Fragment 129

ἔμεθεν δ' ἔχησθα
λάθαν

You've been quiet, girl,
and I feel hungry, but
before I leave,
before I throw away
an almost-rotten peach whose fuzz
no longer tickles my tongue,
I would take you, cutting deep
into the pink flesh of a fruit
too sweet for every day.
But you have forgotten me.

Fragment 168b

ἔγο δὲ μόνα
κατεύδω

And I lie down alone
as time spins and I
do too: too much wine
brings hateful kindness to me,
enough can loosen my lips,
another cup undoes my belt,
one more has the heat
of lust—wine and shame
are a triangle of emotion.
But I loved this vintage
too much, and the friend
in whose bed I hoped
to wake up tomorrow morning
has left after a kiss
fell on someone else's lips
and left mine tasting grapes.

Fragment 88 φιλήσω

I will love the orange blossoms
brought here by merchants—

the pepper's heat—an oil
so strong for such a small black seed
showing passion in size;

cardamom in goat's milk
boiled with honey,
sweeter than wine:

vines' plump grapes
whose mild tang
wakes up my tongue.

Less enticing things
I will also love:
dark fermented fish paste,

bitter bark, rough cloth,
bee stings, nettles
and hard beds.

Because you felt
them all once,
I will love them.

Fragment 24

πόλλα μὲν γὰρ καὶ
κάλα

Like the hand-thrown pots
that line the gymnasium at Sardis,

the columns at the Virgin's temple in Athens,
tall and graceful,

my loves stand together like the Muses,
many and beautiful.

Fragment 120

ἀλλ' ἀβάκην τὰν
φρέν' ἔχω

Some would have me sing curses to old lovers,
but I have a gentle heart; I'll look for other lips.

Fragment 67   ἐφίλησ

I told myself I'd stop
loving just to fill my mind
with the erotic nectar of anticipation.

I said my eyes would only see
the beauty of others,
not wanting what I didn't have.

She was once angry with me
for saying two words too much:
"I want."
I swore I did not love,
but again the thrill is much too near.
I swore I would not love

till now.

Cincinnati native Jordi Alonso is a 2014 graduate of Kenyon College, where he majored in English with a Creative Writing emphasis.

Honeyvoiced, Jordi's first book, comprises poems inspired by the ancient Greek poet Sappho. Because few of Sappho's verses remain intact, he constructed this long series of original poems based on the recovered fragments. Attracted to the sensuality of her work and her food imagery, he made use of those characteristic themes in these derivative poems. To understand Sappho's fragments as clearly as possible, Jordi taught himself ancient Greek; his embrace of languages began with a bilingual Spanish-English childhood and fluency in French. He has also studied Latin and Anglo-Saxon.

Sappho's fragments are not Jordi's only influence. He cites American poets H.D., Edna St. Vincent Millay, Billy Collins, and Melissa Stein as shapers of his poetic interests. He attended the 2013 Southampton Writers Conference for a workshop with Heather McHugh, and also took a workshop with Billy Collins at the 2012 Conference.

Jordi Alonso has published poems in the Portland Review, Pegasus, the Southampton Review, Dovetails, The Lyric, Mountain Gazette, and NEAT Magazine, as well as in the Tupelo Press 30/30 Project. He is currently living on Long Island, New York, pursuing an MFA at Stony Brook Southampton University, where was named the Creative Writing program's first Turner Fellowship winner.

www.ingramcontent.com/pod-product-compliance
Lightning Source LLC
Chambersburg PA
CBHW070944080526
44587CB00015B/2213